The Ultimate *Cheetah* Book for Kids

100+ Amazing Cheetah Facts, Photos & More

Jenny Kellett

BELLANOVA
MELBOURNE · SOFIA · BERLIN

© © 2026 by Jenny Kellett

Cheetahs: The Ultimate Cheetah Book
www.bellanovabooks.com

ISBN: 9786199221969
Imprint: Bellanova Books

All rights reserved. No part of this book may be reproduced in any form by any electronic or mechanical means including photocopying, recording, or information storage and retrieval without permission in writing from the author.

Contents

Introduction 4
Cheetahs - The Basics 6
Characteristics 12
Their Daily Lives 26
Subspecies of cheetah 42
    Southeast African 44
    Asiatic 48
    Northeast African 50
    Northwest African 54
    King Cheetah 56
From Birth to Adulthood 58
Cheetahs and Humans 74
Cheetah Conservation 82
Cheetah Quiz 86
    Answers 90
Word search 92
Sources 95

Introduction

The cheetah's beautiful spotted coat and fast-as-lightning speed makes it one of the world's most beloved felines. But, cheetahs aren't just large cats—they are a fascinating and remarkable species.

In this book, you'll learn more about the different species of cheetah, what makes them so unique, and the problems they face. At the end, test your knowledge in our cheetah quiz. But no cheet-ing, ok?!

Are you ready? *Let's go!*

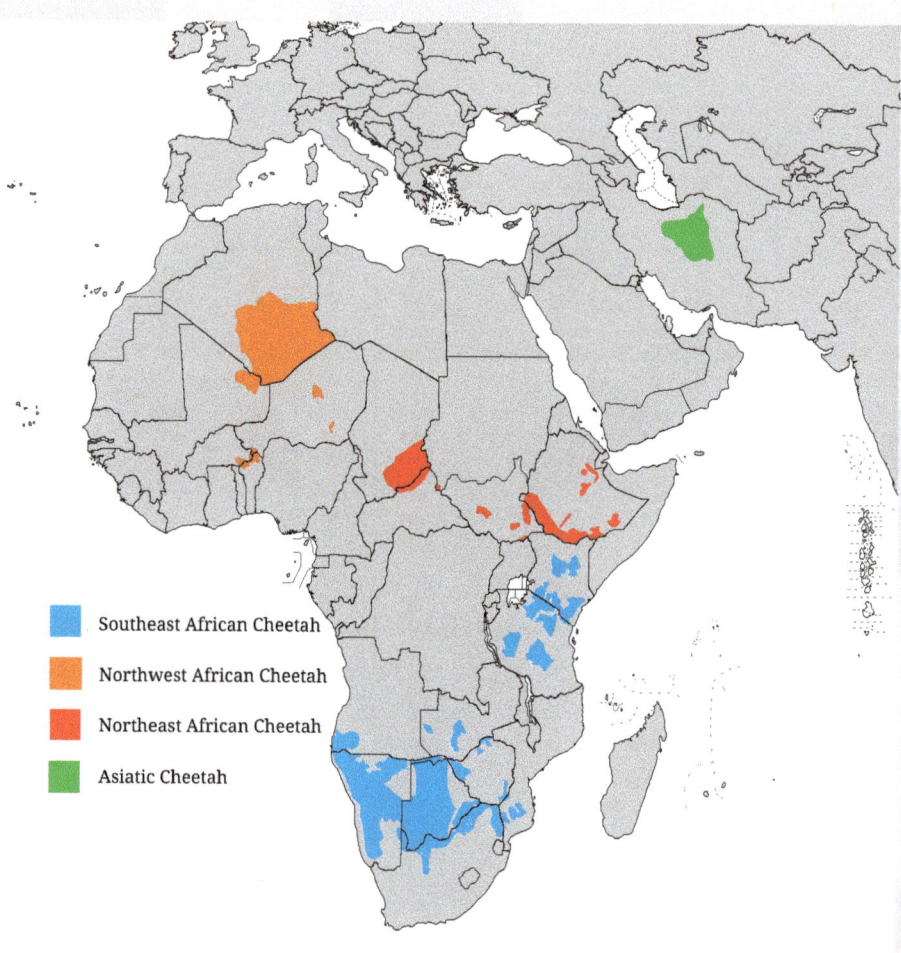

The range of cheetahs, by subspecies.

© *Mario Massone*

Cheetahs: The Basics

What are cheetahs and where do they live?

Cheetahs are large cats that live across 29 African countries and a small population in central Iran. In the 19th century, cheetahs lived in 38 African countries and much of the Middle East and Central India, but sadly their numbers are declining.

The cheetah's closest relatives are the cougar and the jaguarundi. These three species are part of the *Puma* family.

The cheetah's scientific name is *Acinonyx jubatus*.

Cheetahs aren't too picky about where they live and are found in many different habitats, including savannahs, mountain ranges and deserts. They can even live happy lives in captivity in very cold countries. Ideally, they look for areas with few predators, plenty of prey and good visibility. They also like open spaces as it's easier to chase their prey.

A recent estimate shows that around 7,100 cheetahs are living in the wild. Sadly, this is less than 10 per cent of the population that existed in 1900.

Cheetahs are now extinct in Asia, except for around 12 living in central Iran.

Cheetahs are listed as vulnerable on the IUCN Red List. This means that they are at risk of extinction.

The Swahili word for cheetah is 'duma'.

The word 'cheetah' comes from the Sanskrit word *Chitra-ya*, which means 'variegated', 'adorned' or 'painted'.

Cheetahs used to be known as the 'hunting leopard', as they were often used by hunters to help catch prey.

There is no particular word for male and female cheetahs; they are simply male cheetahs and female cheetahs!

International Cheetah Day is celebrated on December 4th every year. On this day, cheetah lovers worldwide raise awareness of the problems that cheetahs face. How will you celebrate?

THE ULTIMATE CHEETAH BOOK

Cheetah **Characteristics**

Size, features, special traits and more.

The main characteristics of cheetahs that set them apart from other large cats are their small heads, short snouts, black tear lines on their faces and long, thin bodies that help them reach their famously fast speeds.

Cheetahs are the fastest land mammals on Earth. They can reach speeds of up to 120 km/h (75 mph), and they can accelerate to 97 km/h (60 mph) in just three seconds!

A Southeast African cheetah on the run in Namibia.

People often get leopards and cheetahs mixed up, but it's easy to tell them apart when you know where to look! For example, leopards have rosettes rather than spots, and they don't have the tear lines that cheetahs have. Cheetahs are also slightly taller than leopards.

Cheetahs are the only cats that are specialised for hunting via long-period chases. Most cats hunt by pouncing and only run short distances.

Cheetahs usually chase for less than one minute over 200-300 m.

As they burn so much energy when they run, cheetahs also need a lot of rest. One study found that cheetahs are actually only moving for around 12 per cent of their day!

Most cheetahs have around 2,000 spots on their coats, each measuring around 3–5 cm (1.2–2.0 in).

No two cheetahs are alike! Like a human fingerprint, you can tell cheetahs apart by their coat patterns.

The cheetah's body is designed to be fast—they have long forelegs that give them a longer stride than most cats. In addition, the bones in their lower legs and feet are very thin and light, and their spines are the longest and most flexible of all cats.

Adult cheetahs have round pupils with orange-yellow irises. Their eyes sit high up on their heads, which helps them keep a lookout over tall grass.

Cheetahs have large nasal passages that help them to take in plenty of oxygen when they are running at high speeds.

Cheetahs have thinner and fewer whiskers than other types of cats.

Cheetahs have quite round-shaped heads, with small ears that are set far apart. Behind their ears, cheetahs have black fur with white markings.

The black lines that run from the inner corner of the cheetah's eyes down its face are called **tear lines**. These vary in size and colour depending on the subspecies.

It is not known what purpose the tear lines serve. However, some scientists believe they help protect cheetahs from the glare of the sun—especially as they usually hunt during the day.

Cheetahs have very long and muscular tails with bushy tufts at the end, either in black or white. The first two-thirds of their tails have spots, while the rest has stripes.

When a cheetah runs, all of its paws are in the air for over half of the time.

A cheetah's claws are always fully extended when they run, allowing them to grip the ground—similar to spikes in a sprinter's shoes. The pads on their feet also have ridges to help with traction.

The cheetah's tail is very long and muscular, which helps it balance when it needs to make quick direction changes during a chase.

Cheetahs have 30 teeth. Their canines are short and flat, which help them to suffocate their prey.

Cheetah paws. Notice their blunt claws, which help them to run faster as they don't get stuck in the ground.
© Marko Kudjerski

In the wild, cheetahs that make it to adulthood live for about seven years. In captivity, it can be 8-12 years. In general, female cheetahs live longer than males.

Cheetahs have blunt **semi-retractable claws** without protective sheaths, the only type of cats to do so.

Although cheetahs vary in size and weight depending on their species, they typically reach 67–94 cm (26–37 in) at the shoulder and weigh between 21 and 72 kg (46 and 159 lb).

Male cheetahs have manes. However they're not nearly as obvious as the lion's, for example. Their mane is usually around 8 cm (3.1 in) long, and the fur is quite rough.

Cheetahs' Daily Lives

What's life like as a cheetah?!

Cheetahs live in three types of social groups: females and their cubs, male-only groups called **coalitions**, and solitary males.

They are not the most sociable cats and they generally try to avoid each other, but they will be friendly enough if they come into contact another cheetah—unless it's during mating season.

A coalition of cheetahs hunting.

Female cheetah with her cub.

Coalitions are usually made up of two to four male cheetahs, often siblings from the same litter. Each coalition has a dominant male.

Female cheetahs are the least sociable and tend to keep to themselves or with their cubs, except when mating.

Female cheetahs aren't territorial. The area they live in is called their **home range**—but this can overlap with other females' without causing any problems. So if they come across another female, they will usually just ignore them and walk away.

A male Southeast African cheetah marking his territory. © Joachim Huber.

Males, on the other hand, start to occupy and defend a territory once they reach around the age of four. They will usually choose their territory based on where there is likely to be lots of females.

Researchers have noticed that sometimes cubs from different females can get mixed up. Fortunately, their new adopted mothers generally don't seem to mind and take them in!

To **mark their territory**, male cheetahs will urinate on trees and termite mounds to warn off other cheetahs.

Catching Dinner: The Cheetah Way

When a cheetah sees a potential meal, it has five different methods for catching their prey:

- **Walk slowly** toward their prey in full view, then break into a sprint when it gets to 60-70 m (200-230 ft) away.
- **Sit and wait** in a crouched position until the prey moves toward them before attacking.
- If their prey is **distracted**, they may start chasing it from as far as 600 m (1,968 ft) away.
- **Stalk** its prey while walking in a crouched position, occasionally freezing until it gets close enough to launch an attack.
- **Flush** its prey out from where it's hiding and then pursue it with a fast chase.

A Southeast African cheetah with its prey.

Once they catch up to their prey, they will trip it over and bite its throat until it suffocates or crush its skull if it is a smaller animal. They will then drag their prey under cover—away from other predators—to eat it.

A cheetah having a clean while it rests.

Male cheetahs that aren't part of a coalition tend to roam over much larger areas, avoiding male territories, and looking for food and females.

Cheetahs are **diurnal** (active during the day); this is because it helps them to avoid competition from other predators, such as leopards and lions, which hunt at night.

However, if a cheetah is living in an area where there isn't much competition for food, or they live in the scorching hot Sahara desert, they are often more active at night.

Due to their lightweight size and build, cheetahs can't defend themselves against larger predators such as lions. Therefore, if a lion tries to steal a cheetah's prey, it will usually just give it up rather than fight for it.

Cheetahs eat their food very quickly to avoid it being stolen by other predators. They can eat up to 14 kg in one sitting if they need to!

Cheetahs usually go to sleep in groups. However, there will always be one cheetah keeping a lookout for predators.

Cheetahs are **carnivores**, meaning they only eat meat. Their favourite food is small- to medium-sized prey such as impala, springbok and gazelles. They may also eat smaller animals such as rats, hares and guinea fowl if they can't find anything bigger. Often, cheetahs in coalitions will attempt to catch larger prey than singletons such as wildebeests.

Cheetahs are mostly active during the day and they have two hunting peaks, usually between 7-10 am and again at 4-7 pm. They'll then usually sleep for the rest of the day.

Cheetahs will drink water every day if it is available but they can go several days without any water. However, in some parts of Africa, they don't always have access to water, so they must live off the water from their food.

Cheetahs usually eat around 2.8 kg (6.2 lb.) of meat per day. They don't always hunt everyday, though—it can be once every two to five days.

A cheetah having a drink at Schönbrunn Zoo in Vienna, Austria.

Cheetah Chats

There are many vocalisations that cheetahs use to communicate with each other. Here are a few of their favourites:

- **Yipping** is a high-pitched barking sound. Adult cheetahs use this sound to locate one another if they get separated. Females will use this sound when they are looking for their cubs.
- **Chirping** sounds like a bird cheeping and is used by cubs when they are lost or stressed.
- **Yelping** is similar to yipping but adult cheetahs use it when they are scared.

- **Churr**, also known as stuttering, is often used during social encounters.
- **Growls, hissing** and **spitting** are used by cheetahs when they are annoyed, scared or in a dangerous situation.
- Cheetahs also **purr** when they're happy. It sounds similar to a domestic cat's purr but much louder!

Cheetahs: Subspecies

There are four **subspecies** of cheetah. The differences are subtle, but each subspecies lives in a different area and has adapted to its environment in unique ways.

Let's take a quick look to see the differences, and afterwards see you if you can work out the subspecies of the cheetahs in this book!

Southeast African Cheetah

Acinonyx jubatus jubatus

The Southeast African cheetah, also known as the **Namibian cheetah**, is the most common cheetah subspecies. Until 2017, this subspecies was divided into two: the eastern and the southern cheetah, but now scientists have agreed that they are so similar that they should be the same subspecies.

It is native to East and Southern Africa, in Angola, Kenya, Botswana, Mozambique, Namibia, South Africa and Zambia.

You can find Southeast African cheetahs in various habitats, including the lowland areas and deserts of the Kalahari desert, farmlands in Namibia and the swampy savannahs of Botswana's Okavango Delta.

The spots on the Southeast African cheetah are denser than on other subspecies— and they have more spots on their faces. Also, look out for their distinct brown "moustaches" and the very white fur on their underbelly.

Despite being the most common cheetah, Southeast African cheetahs still face many risks from human activity, and they have already gone extinct in Malawi, Lesotho and the Democratic Republic of Congo.

Asiatic Cheetah

Acinonyx jubatus venaticus

The Asiatic cheetah is a **critically endangered** subspecies that lives in central Iran. It is the only subspecies of the cheetah that still lives in Asia. Sadly, as of 2022, only 12 individuals are believed to live in the wild—nine males and three females. As their future is so fragile, they live in remote protected areas where there is little human activity.

The Asiatic cheetah is distinctive thanks to its mane and coat, which are shorter than the African subspecies.

Asiatic cheetah in Iran. © *Tehran Times.*

Their fur is a buff-to-light fawn colour, which is paler on the sides, below the eye, on the inner legs and at the front of the muzzle.

Asiatic cheetahs have lines of small black spots on their heads and neck, while the rest of the body has irregularly placed spots, and the tips of their tails have black stripes.

Northeast African Cheetah

Acinonyx jubatus soemmeringii

The Northeast African cheetah, also known as the Sudan or Central African cheetah, lives in South Sudan and Ethiopia. They live in sparse populations in open habitats such as grasslands and savannahs. There are an estimated 950 left in the wild.

Like the Southeast African cheetah, the Sudan cheetah is quite large with a densely spotted coat. Compared to other African cheetahs, its coat is thicker and coarser, and its belly fur is the darkest— sometimes with some black spots.

Northeast African cheetah.
© William Warby

Northeast African cheetahs have the largest head size of all subspecies, and they don't have moustache markings like their southern neighbour.

Most Northeast African cheetahs have no spots on their hind feet, which is one of the best ways to tell them apart from the Southeast African cheetah. You will also notice distinct white patches around its eyes. They have thick tails, and the tips can be either black or white.

When they are kept in captivity in cold countries, Northeast African cheetahs develop fluffy winter coats, unlike any other type of African cheetah.

Northwest African Cheetah

Acinonyx jubatus hecki

The Northwest African cheetah, also known as the Saharan cheetah, is a **critically endangered** subspecies that lives in small populations across Algeria, Benin, Burkina Faso, Mali and Niger. There are less than 250 left in the wild.

Compared to other cheetahs, the Northwest African cheetah is very unique. It has a short coat that is nearly white with spots that fade from black along the spine to light brown on the legs. They have few spots on their faces and are often missing the tear marks that help make cheetahs so distinct. Their faces are also thinner and more dog-like than other species.

Northwest African cheetah. © *Steve Wilson*

Northwest African cheetahs are smaller than other species. They have adapted to living in the hot Saharan desert where there is very little water. Unlike other cheetahs, they are mostly active at night, to avoid the heat of the day. They also need to travel longer distances than other cheetahs to find food.

KING CHEETAH

The king cheetah is a rare cheetah that lives in southern Africa. While not officially a subspecies, it is incredibly beautiful and distinct.

Due to a genetic fur mutation, it has three thick black stripes along its back and large black blotchy spots, making it very unique.

It is believed there are no more than 10 in the wild and around 50 in captivity.

King cheetah. Do you notice the very unique markings? © *Olga Ernst*

From birth to adulthood

Baby cheetahs are some of the most adorable in the animal world, so let's learn more about their early lives.

Baby cheetahs are called **cubs**.

Cheetahs have three life stages: cub (birth to 18 months), adolescence (18-24 months), and adulthood (24 months+).

Cheetahs' **gestation period** (how long the pregnancy lasts) is around three months (90-95 days). They breed throughout the year and usually have litters of between three to four cubs—although it can be up to eight.

When they are born, cheetah cubs' eyes are shut; they open after four to 11 days. Then, after around two weeks, cubs start walking.

Cheetah cubs are born with adorable fluffy mohawk-like tufts covering their neck and back called a **mantle**.

Scientists believe cubs' mantles help camouflage them from predators. They start to lose their mantle at around three months old.

Cubs start getting their milk teeth when they are between 3-6 years old. These are replaced by adult teeth at around eight months old.

Cheetah cubs born in the wild weigh 150–300 g (5.3–10.6 oz) at birth, while those born in captivity usually weigh around 500 g (18 oz). Cheetahs in captivity have easier access to quality food, so the mothers can focus on self-care rather than hunting—meaning their cubs are larger.

Rare Northwest cheetah cub. © *Steve Wilson*

Although cubs are born with their unique spots, their coat appears much darker as the spots are all squashed together. Their spots spread out as they grow, and their coat becomes lighter.

Newborn cubs will often spit a lot!

Cubs are very playful, especially once they reach four months old. They love wrestling with each other, climbing trees and practicing hunting on small animals.

It's a tough life for cheetah cubs as they are often preyed upon by animals such as hyenas and lions. However, their mothers do their best to keep them safe. They keep their cubs well hidden in a **lair** for the first two months and only feed them during the early morning. She never goes far away and moves her cubs to a new location every five to six days.

Cubs start coming out of their lair and experiencing life as a grown-up cheetah when they are two months old. They will learn how to hunt and look out for predators and may even catch their own small prey such as hares when they are six months old, but they don't go out hunting on their own until they are around 12 months old.

The survival rate of cubs ranges from 17-to 70%. In areas such as the Serengeti National Park, where there are lots of large predators, the survival rate is very low. However, in the Namibian farmlands, where cheetahs are the main predator, their survival rate is much higher.

Cubs drink their mother's milk until they are around four months old, but their mothers will slowly introduce them to meat after two months.

Young female cheetahs will often stay close to their mothers for life, while the males go off on their own or form a coalition. Coalitions are usually made up of siblings.

Female cheetahs can start having cubs between 2-3 years old. After they give birth, they can get pregnant again 17-20 months later.

Once they are around 20 months old, cubs are usually very independent. They reach full adult size between 49-96 months of age.

Southeast African cheetah and her cub.

Cheetahs and Humans

We may be very different, but we all share the same planet. So how well do we get along?

The earliest known human drawings of cheetahs, found in caves in France, date back to 32,000–26,000 BC.

In the past, cheetahs were kept as pets by the rich and powerful—pharaohs, kings, and emperors would keep cheetahs as a sign of wealth and status.

Cheetahs have been tamed by humans for thousands of years, however they have never been domesticated like cats.

Ancient Egyptians *loved* cheetahs and treated them like royalty. They even believed a cat goddess named Mafdet, often pictured with a cheetah's head, would help speed the pharaoh's soul to the afterworld.

There are strict regulations on keeping cheetahs as pets in the USA and other countries; however, it is not uncommon for the wealthy to own a cheetah in the United Arab Emirates.

THE ULTIMATE CHEETAH BOOK

Cheetah at Whipsnade Zoo, London.
© Bernard Dupont.

The first cheetah brought into captivity was at the Zoological Society of London in 1829.

Cheetahs are the least dangerous of the large cats. They are more likely to run away from humans than attack them, because they don't see them as prey.

During the seventh century AD, cheetahs were used by the nobility in the Middle East for hunting. The cheetahs would have a special seat on the back of the saddle of the hunters' horse.

THE ULTIMATE CHEETAH BOOK

The Romans called cheetahs *leopardos*, as they believed they were a mix between a leopard and a lion due to the fluffy mantles seen on cheetah cubs.

If you enjoy reading, you'll love the book *How It Was with Dooms*. It's a true story about a Kenyan family that raised an orphaned cheetah cub named Duma. Two films, *Cheetah* (1989) and *Duma* (2005), were inspired by the book.

Two South African rugby union teams, *The Toyota Free State Cheetahs* and *The Cheetahs* have a running cheetah as their emblem.

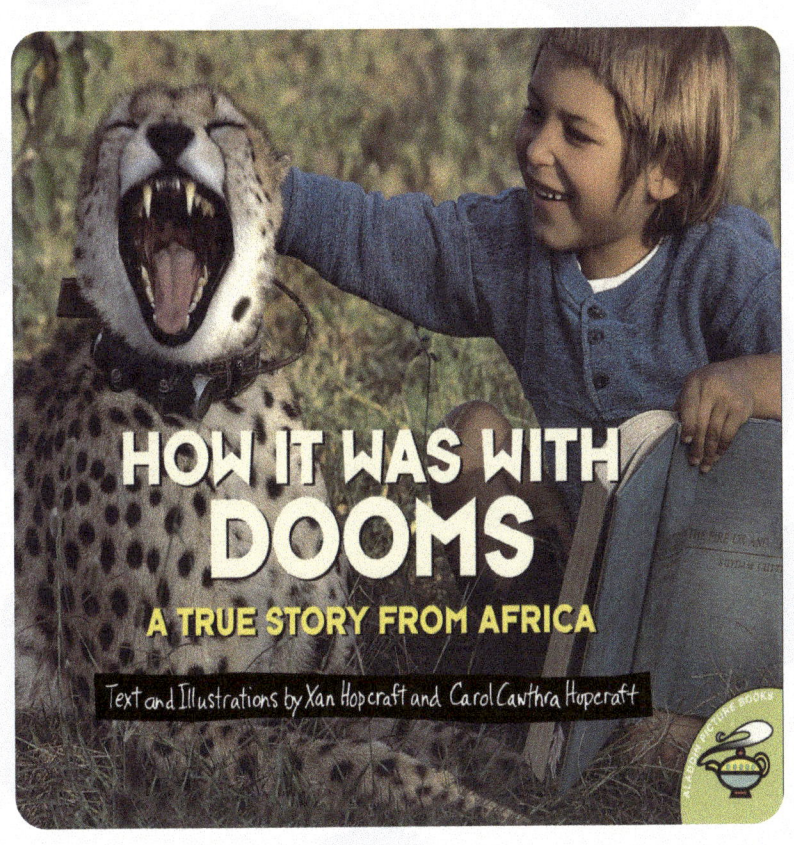

© Simon and Schuster.

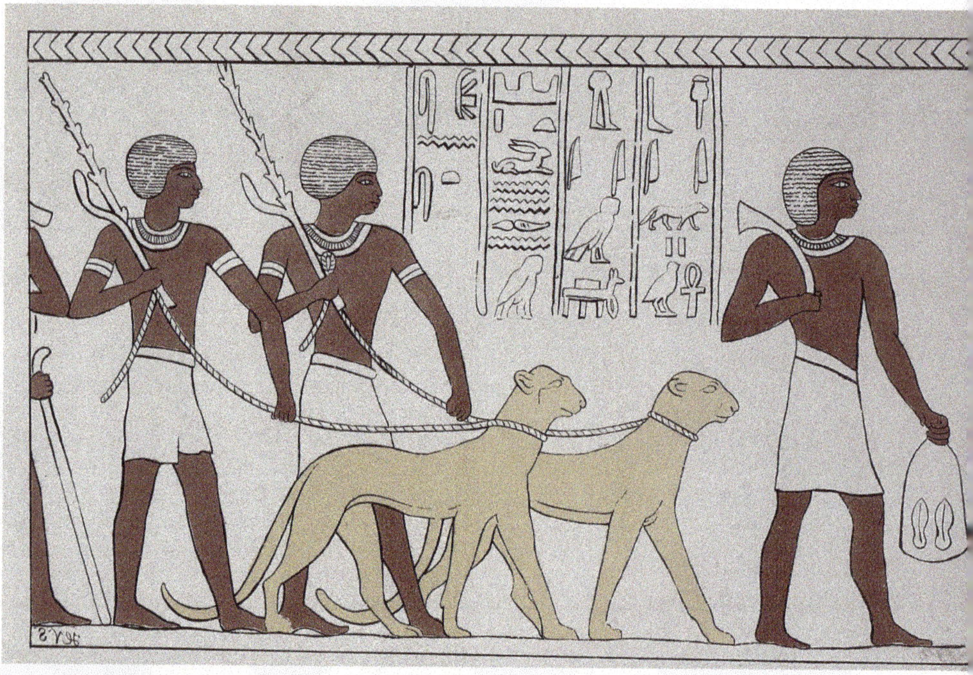

A depiction of Ancient Egyptians with cheetahs. © *Wellcome Images.*

The animated television series *Thundercats*, features a character named Cheetara, a cheetah.

Perhaps one of the most famous cheetahs in the world is Chester Cheetah, of Cheetos fame! He became the orange snacks' mascot in 1985.

Cheetah, a fictional character from DC Comics, is one of Wonder Woman's biggest enemies.

Cheetah
CONSERVATION

Sadly, cheetahs have a difficult and uncertain future. The cheetah species as a whole is considered to be endangered, while two subspecies—Northwest African and Asiatic—are critically endangered.

The cheetah faces many challenges, including hunting, predation, the illegal pet trade, climate change and loss of habitat. Many of these causes are human.

As their numbers decrease, their populations become more spread out, making it harder for cheetahs to find a mate, leading to **inbreeding**. Inbreeding makes cheetahs more vulnerable to a range of diseases.

Fortunately, there are thousands of cheetah lovers and organisations around the world that are working hard to protect the cheetah's future.

How can *you* help cheetahs?

Cheetahs need help from people just like you to raise awareness of their problems.

You can support many organisations, including *The Cheetah Conservation Fund, WWF, African Wildlife Foundation*, and the *Cheetah Conservation Botswana*.

Through these organisations, you have opportunities to adopt a cheetah, donate money and learn more about other ways you can help.

A little goes a long way. Here are a few ideas:

- Instead of gifts on your birthday, ask your friends and family for donations to your favourite cheetah charity.
- Hold a bake sale to raise money.
- Be a cheetah ambassador! Share information about the problems cheetahs face on your social media and speak to friends and family to spread the word.
- Use the hashtag **#SaveTheCheetah** on social media.
- Adopt a cheetah (virtually, of course!) through the organisations mentioned above.
- Check with your local zoo to see what projects they're involved in and how you can help.

CHEETAH QUIZ

Now test your knowledge in our cheetah quiz! Answers are on page 90.

1 Can you name the four subspecies of cheetah?

2 Which two continents do cheetahs live on in the wild?

3 Do you know the cheetah's scientific name?

4 How many cheetahs are living in the wild?

5 What are cheetahs listed as by the IUCN?

6   When is International Cheetah Day celebrated?

7   How many spots do most cheetahs have on their coats?

8   Cheetah siblings have the same spot patterns. True or false?

9   How many teeth do cheetahs have?

10 What are the black lines that run down a cheetahs face called?

11 What is a group of male cheetahs called?

12 Cheetahs are herbivores. True or false?

13 What sound do cubs make if they are lost or stressed?

14 Which subspecies of cheetah is the most common?

15 How many Asiatic cheetahs are known to live in the wild?

16 Which species of cheetah has the largest head?

17 How long is the cheetah's gestation period?

18 What is a mantle?

19 When do cubs start walking?

20 Cheetahs often attack humans. True or false?

Answers

1. Southeast African, Asiatic, Northeast African and Northwest African.
2. Africa and Asia.
3. *Acinonyx jubatus*.
4. Around 7,100
5. Vulnerable.
6. December 4th.
7. Around 2,000.
8. False. No two cheetahs are alike.
9. 30.
10. Tear lines.
11. A coalition.
12. False. They are carnivores.
13. Chirping.
14. Southeast African cheetah.
15. 12.
16. The Northeast African cheetah.
17. 90-95 days.
18. The tufts of hair that cheetah cubs have.
19. After two weeks.
20. False.

Cheetahs
WORD SEARCH

W	E	D	S	A	C	H	E	E	T	A	H
B	V	N	S	J	Y	T	E	G	F	S	S
P	O	Y	D	D	S	B	J	M	S	I	C
J	Y	R	M	A	M	M	A	L	S	A	O
A	H	G	D	E	N	V	N	Y	R	T	A
F	B	R	S	C	A	G	F	E	J	I	L
J	E	G	F	U	D	S	E	A	E	C	I
M	J	L	F	B	D	S	R	R	B	E	T
Q	W	Z	I	S	P	O	T	T	E	D	I
G	N	V	C	N	X	D	E	O	F	D	O
L	J	G	P	R	E	D	A	T	O	R	N
M	N	R	U	T	E	Q	Z	D	W	E	F

Can you find all the words below in the word search puzzle on the left?

CHEETAH   MAMMALS   COALITION

ASIATIC   ENDANGERED   CUBS

FELINE   SPOTTED   PREDATOR

THE ULTIMATE CHEETAH BOOK

Word search solution

	E			C	H	E	E	T	A	H
		N							S	
			D					I		C
			M	A	M	M	A	L	S	A	O
				N					T	A
F			C		G				I	L
	E		U			E			C	I
		L		B			R			T
			I	S	P	O	T	T	E	D	I
				N					D	O
			P	R	E	D	A	T	O	R	N

Sources

Southeast African cheetah - Wikipedia (2019). Available at: https://en.wikipedia.org/wiki/Southeast_African_cheetah (Accessed: 29 April 2022).

(2022) Education.nationalgeographic.org. Available at: https://education.nationalgeographic.org/resource/cheetahs-brink-extinction-again (Accessed: 27 May 2022).

Everything You Need to Know About Pet Cheetahs (2022). Available at: https://pethelpful.com/exotic-pets/about-pet-cheetahs (Accessed: 27 May 2022).

Northwest African cheetah - Wikipedia (2022). Available at: https://en.wikipedia.org/wiki/Northwest_African_cheetah (Accessed: 27 May 2022).

The Elvis of Cheetahs (2022). Available at: https://www.awf.org/blog/elvis-cheetahs (Accessed: 27 May 2022).

Carnivores, S. (2020) Claws - Animal Experiences At Wingham Wildlife Park In Kent, Animal Experiences At Wingham Wildlife Park In Kent. Available at: https://winghamwildlifepark.co.uk/claws (Accessed: 29 May 2022).

14 Cute Baby Cheetah Facts: Diet, Cub Sounds, Photos (2021). Available at: https://storyteller.travel/baby-cheetah/ (Accessed: 29 May 2022).

Cheetah (character) - Wikipedia (2022). Available at: https://en.wikipedia.org/wiki/Cheetah_(character) (Accessed: 29 May 2022).

International Cheetah Day - Cheetah Conservation

Fund Canada (2022). Available at: https://cheetah.org/canada/events/international-cheetah-day-2/ (Accessed: 29 May 2022).

10 things you didn't know about cheetahs (2022). Available at: https://www.zsl.org/blogs/wild-about/10-things-you-didnt-know-about-cheetahs (Accessed: 29 May 2022).

CHEETAH CONSERVATION BOTSWANA (2022). Available at: https://www.cheetahconservationbotswana.org/ (Accessed: 1 June 2022).

Homepage • Cheetah Conservation Fund (2022). Available at: https://cheetah.org/ (Accessed: 1 June 2022).

We hope you learned some awesome facts about cheetahs!

Which was your favourite? Let us know in a review!

Visit us at www.bellanovabooks.com for more great books.

ALSO BY JENNY KELLETT

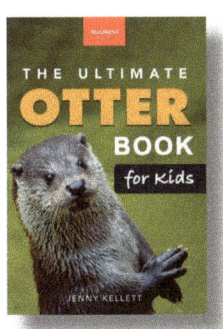 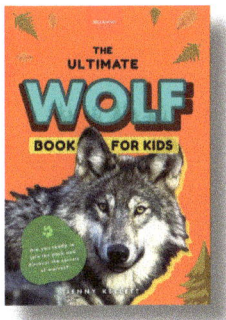 

... and more!

Available at

www.bellanovabooks.com

and all major online bookstores.

www.ingramcontent.com/pod-product-compliance
Lightning Source LLC
La Vergne TN
LVHW050843080526
838202LV00010B/325